IN YOUR DREAMS

RECOGNIZING GOD AT WORK
WHILE YOU SLEEP

Melinda Eye Cooper

New Harbor Press
Rapid City, SD

New Harbor Press
1601 Mt Rushmore Rd, Ste 3288
Rapid City, SD 57701
www.newharborpress.com

Ordering Information:
Quantity sales. Special discounts are available on quantity purchases by corporations, associations, and others. For details, contact the "Special Sales Department" at the address above.

In Your Dreams/Cooper —1st ed.

ISBN 978-1-63357-471-7

First edition: 10 9 8 7 6 5 4 3 2 1

Contents

Introduction

I will praise the LORD, who counsels me; even at night my heart instructs me. (Psalm 16:7 NIV)

Why did I dream *that?*
Sometimes, we have the strangest dreams. During the day, our thoughts were not on that subject. If so, the dream would make sense. As a matter of fact, the content of the dream seems to be from left field and is the furthest thing from our minds.

These types of dreams have captivated me for most of my life.

I'd love to say I have a degree in Psychology and have expertise in this field, but I don't. I wish I'd studied it earlier in life, but I didn't. What I have is my own life experience, what God has revealed, and what I've learned along the way to share with others.

Dreams have affected my life so much they've *changed* me.

It was in this "changing" that I discovered a thing or two. Interesting things about how God works in our lives. My first impactful dream was when I was eleven years old. The bad dream drove me to share it with my dad.

Interestingly, I didn't know what it meant until many, many years later. And I thought about it for over forty years.

Here is that dream (italics below):

I walked up front in the little church I grew up in to join. I was facing the church pews from where the pulpit was, and my dad (though I didn't see him in the dream, I discerned his presence) would have been standing as the pastor of our little church. There were three older ladies in one church pew facing me. They were sisters. One of the sisters (and I vividly recall which one) was sort of smirking or giggling at the fact that I wanted to join the church. Then she threw a rock and hit me in the eye.

I woke up horrified. I loved these older sisters in my church. Why would one of them laugh and throw a rock at me? Dad listened to my dream with great interest, and his first question after hearing the details was "Which eye?" I tried to remember but wasn't certain. Maybe it was my right eye? He said the eye had significance but didn't know why she'd throw a rock at me.

I'll come back to this short dream at the end of this book because how God revealed the meaning of the dream stunned me. He used dreams to "bookend" a spiritual breakthrough in my life and completely blew my mind.

But this short childhood dream is a good example of a dream given to get attention. It worked well. I've never forgotten it and never will.

The question is, "Have *you* ever awoken mesmerized by an incredible dream? Or sat up in bed terrified, only to realize it was just a bad dream?" I imagine so, and maybe that's the reason you've chosen to read this book.

The truth is, everyone dreams. They're important for our mental well-being. We must sort out the events of our day and deal with them. The issue is that some of us don't remember them well. Others do but chalk it up as just a weird dream. They get started with their day and the dream evaporates like steam from a hot cup of coffee.

Often, I tell my husband about my strange dreams. Ninety percent of the time, he replies, "I didn't dream."

I'm a light sleeper and he's a heavy sleeper. At times in the middle of the night, I hear him making sounds in his sleep or moving his legs around in bed. I know he's dreaming. So, I nudge him to wake him up and ask about the dream. He rouses and quickly remembers what was happening in the dream almost every time.

But after he slept all night and snoozed the alarm a few times, he forgets his dreams and doesn't even think he dreamed at all.

Truthfully, we've been taught to disregard dreams. As parents, we calm our children and say, "It was just a dream." When we grow older and mention our crazy dreams, people may seem interested, but we worry they think we're off our rocker.

But in the spiritual realm with God communicating in this way, dreams shouldn't be disregarded. They can be quite important. Some of them are part of the transformation process as we become more like Christ in our Christian journey. If we pay close attention and ponder them in this way, we'll see God working while we're sleeping.

Christians have been filled with the Holy Spirit. Our bodies rest, but God within us doesn't stop His work just because we need some sleep.

He uses dreams to draw us into a deeper relationship with Him.

"Why?" We may ask if we don't know Him well yet.

Why not?

The truth is, God will use anything and everything to draw us into a closer, more mature relationship with Him. Even our bad life experiences will be used for good purposes.

Because of His deep love for us, the work is constant. Even while we're unaware, unconscious, and sleeping.

His ways are perfect.

CHAPTER ONE

Does God Speak in Dreams?

For God does speak—now one way—now another, though no one perceives it.

In a dream, in a vision of the night, when deep sleep falls on people as they slumber in their beds, he may speak in their ears and terrify them with warnings, to turn them away from their wrongdoing and keep them from pride, to preserve them from the pit, their lives from perishing from the sword. (Job 33:14–18 NIV)

Why does God give dreams?

This Scripture speaks volumes about why God gives dreams. He knows us well. Often, we don't listen like we should. We're selfish, hardheaded, and sinful. Yet, He loves us. God cares about the smallest details of our lives and desires an intimate relationship with us. Dreams are personal. Most often, the dream from God is for us, about us, or involves us in some way.

We see many reasons in Job 33:14–18 to answer our question:

- God speaks, yet no one perceives it.
- God terrifies us with warnings.
- God wants us to turn from our wrongdoing.
- God wants to keep us from pride.
- God wants to preserve us from the pit.
- God wants to keep our lives from perishing.

God is working *while* we sleep. He's giving us dreams to get us going in the right direction or keep us from moving in the wrong direction. He's drawing us into a deeper relationship with Him, to make us Holy, humble, and more like Jesus.

If you've never read the Bible, or studied it much, you may be surprised to learn the Bible is full of verses about dreams and night visions. Genesis mentions dreams more than any other book. I find it interesting that in Genesis, the word *"dream"* is mentioned thirty-two times, and the word *"pray"* is only mentioned eight times. It shows God speaking through dreams more than others went to God in prayer (at least in Genesis). I wonder if this ratio is the same today, and we don't realize God is speaking in this way.

If we search the Bible for dreams, we'll find plenty.

Genesis:

- Abimelech dreamed. (Genesis 20:1–3)
- Jacob dreamed. (Genesis 28:10–12)
- Laban dreamed. (Genesis 21:34)
- Joseph dreamed. (Genesis 31:9–11)
- Pharaoh dreamed. (Genesis 41:1–3, 5–7)

Judges:

- Gideon hears a dream and an interpretation of the dream. (Judges 7:13, 15)

1 Kings:

- Solomon dreamed. (1 Kings 3:5)

Daniel:

- Daniel dreamed. He could understand visions and dreams of all kinds. (Daniel 1:17)
- Nebuchadnezzar dreamed. (Daniel 2:1, 4:4)

Joel:

- "And afterward, I will pour out my Spirit on all people. Your sons and daughters will prophesy, your old men will dream dreams, your young men will see visions." (Joel 2:28)

Matthew:

- God gave Joseph dreams about Jesus and Mary, when to go away and when to come back. (Matthew 1:20; 2:12–13, 22)
- Pilate's wife dreamed Jesus was innocent. (Matthew 27:19)

The Bible is "flavored" with dreams and night visions like a steak is seasoned with salt and pepper. If they weren't important, they wouldn't be there.

Most of us who have children will testify each child is unique and special. The same is true in our relationship with God. We're all a bit different and how He chooses to reveal Himself to each of us can also be unique. He speaks specifically about things of concern, like making us aware of something coming up or revealing a sin we're unaware of in our waking life.

Giving dreams is one way God reveals truth.

When we become familiar with His ways, we'll begin to understand which dreams have meaning. Some dreams are simply our minds downloading events of the day into storage. They help us sort out the emotions and internal conflicts we experienced during our waking hours.

In the next chapters, I'll share my dream insights. You can then begin to ponder your dream life and see if anything clicks in your relationship with God.

Is He revealing sin through a repetitive dream you often ponder? Is He warning you about something coming up around the corner? Does He want you free from bondage, and you're unaware of the *chains* binding you?

If we pay close attention and consider the dream meaning from a different perspective, some incredible change can take place. But we must be willing to seek God in this area of our lives.

There are different types of dreams God may use. He can do anything He pleases, as we well know.

The *key* to unlocking truth in our spiritual life will come when we begin to take note of the dreams, ponder them, and ask God to reveal meaning. The keys I found through different types of dreams deepened my relationship with God in *powerful* ways. Though I'm confident there are many more, here are a few types of dreams God may use:

1. **Prophetic:** Shows us future events in life.
2. **Symbolic:** Strange pictures or events.
3. **Sin Revelation:** Dreams (almost always recurring) showing us sin we are unaware of in our waking hours.
4. **Testing:** Questions us in dreams to find out our honest and true reaction.
5. **Bondage Breaking:** Dreams (almost always recurring) showing us an area of our lives in which we are bound, and God wants us FREE.

One thing found in many dream books is a glossary at the back listing dream symbols and their meanings. To be honest, I've looked up countless symbols over the years.

But with great confidence, I can say most dreams given by God cannot be interpreted in this way. What He's showing often pertains to our **personal** lives. They're not in a list of universal symbols that each of us could individually relate. Though there's no harm in seeking meaning in a glossary of a dream book. There may be a *hint* found there, but the true meaning may take years to play out or even to understand why God would give such a dream.

God's work is deeper than a universal symbol at the back of a dream book. His work is vital to our spiritual growth. The dreams are meant to change us in our waking life, and they will eventually, when we understand how God is working while we're sleeping.

One truth is most sin-recognition dreams are given in areas of our lives where we do not believe we're guilty of the sin. In our waking life, we think we're good. We're not thieves, murderers, or adulterers. We're not bowing down and worshipping an idol.

But God knows better. He wants us to see the sin, recognize the error of our ways, and turn away from it.

> *"Teacher, which is the greatest commandment in the Law?" Jesus replied: "Love the Lord your God with all your **heart** and with all your **soul** and with all your **mind**.' This is the first and greatest commandment. And the second is like it: 'Love your neighbor as yourself.' All the Law and the Prophets hang on these two commandments." (Matthew 22:36–40 NIV)*

The work of God in our dreams is ultimately to change our hearts, souls, and minds. God uses dreams to change how we feel and what we love. He changes our perceptions of reality through prophetic dreams. He changes our thinking from earthly to enlightened.

We *will* love God with all our heart, soul, and mind. He works at a subconscious level, speaking through dreams to change us.

He spoke the world into existence.

His words (even though often it is pictures in our dreams) are one way He's speaking our spiritual growth into existence.

He is changing us. One dream at a time.

We will love Him with all our *heart*. We will love Him with all our *soul*. And we will love Him with all our *mind*.

Does God **speak** in dreams?

Of course, let's learn more.

Part One

The Heart

CHAPTER TWO

Sin Revelation
(Through Recurring Dreams)

*"If the whole Israelite community sins unintention-
ally and does what is forbidden in any of the Lord's
commands, even though the community is unaware
of the matter, when they realize their guilt and the
sin they committed becomes known, the assembly
must bring a young bull as a sin offering and present it before the tent of meeting." (Leviticus 4:13–14
NIV)*

There's no question that God wants us to turn away from
our wrongdoing.

It's all over the Bible. It's the main reason Jesus came and
paid our sin debt in full on the cross. (Thank goodness!)

Unfortunately, we're incapable of being sinless due to our
fallen nature. We're flesh and blood—prone to sin in most every
way. Even when we try our best, we still do. Our thoughts are
bad enough to get us into trouble without the actions that often
follow.

In the referenced Scripture found in Leviticus, we see the
community *unaware* of a specific sin. But when they realize their

guilt, and the sin they committed becomes known, then an offering had to be made for that unknown sin.

In our lives, we're also sometimes unaware of our sin. We think we're doing good. We don't do the obvious sins. We don't lie. We honor our parents. We haven't committed adultery or murder. But sin runs deep in our veins.

> "You have heard that it was said, 'You shall not commit adultery.' But I tell you that anyone who looks at a woman lustfully has already committed adultery with her in his heart. (Matthew 5:27–28 NIV)

Jesus said even looking at another with lust is the same as adultery. So, when we consider sin the way Jesus explained it, we're all going to struggle.

God must do the work within us through the power of the Holy Spirit to make us aware and then remove it. When He completes the job with one sin, He'll move to the next spiritual work needed while we linger in our flesh.

When God reveals sin to us through a series of dreams, we will eventually repent. With connection comes conviction. No question about it, when we're **convicted** by the Holy Spirit and the sin **connection** is made in our waking life, we want to turn away from it.

But often, we don't know we're sinning. This can be for a variety of reasons. It can be a sin we picked up in childhood through how we were raised, and we keep toting it around well into our adult years. We never considered it to be a problem in our relationship with God.

If you've ever read Leviticus, you may understand just how many sins we commit in complete unawareness. Something may slowly become an idol, and we're clueless.

God will bring it to our attention one way or another. He won't allow anyone or anything to take His place in our lives. It might take some time, but eventually, the idol will come crashing down.

In my personal experience, He's been working during my waking hours, testing me, and still working in my sleep with dreams, revealing my sin. Trying to get me to recognize the sin so I'll turn away from it and change how I *think* about it.

In Job 33:15–18, we discover how much God wants to help us in our lives. He wants us to turn from our wrongdoing. He wants to save us from perishing. How wonderful is someone who continues to work while we rest?

I'm reminded of a baby peacefully snoozing away while Mom is up working. She's cleaning the house, cooking dinner, and doing laundry. He's unaware she's doing all the work. He's getting the sleep his little body needs to grow, but she's taking advantage of his downtime to get some work done for *his* benefit.

Here is a great example of a sin revelation God brought to my attention through recurring dreams.

During this time of my life, my husband and I were raising three young boys (approximately 2004). We didn't have a lot of extra money. So I was careful with spending. It seemed we couldn't save a dime. If we did manage to save some money, then some unexpected expense would come up and we had to spend it. We got used to stretching a dollar, and these life circumstances went on for years.

At some point, I began having a similar dream.

> *Someone has stolen my wallet or purse. Or I have my wallet, but it's empty. Someone has stolen my debit card or cash. I panic and begin searching for my money or wallet. I see a glimpse of the person who took it, and I chase the thief, but can't catch them. I'm in a terrible state because someone has stolen my money.*

I'd wake up frustrated and felt violated because of the theft.

During my waking hours, some testing was also taking place in my day-to-day life.

Here is an example of what I mean:

Once, at a local gas station, I put ten dollars of gasoline in my car. I wrote a check for that amount and went inside to pay. The cashier took the check, initialed it, and placed it in the cash drawer. Then she began counting out cash and handed me ninety dollars. I held the money in my hand—credulous and confused.

She had no idea how tempting it was to be handed ninety dollars in cash. We were flat broke. It was a lot of money (at the time) and could have paid a bill. But there was no way I could have kept it in good conscience.

"I'm sorry," I said as I handed the cash back. "My check was for ten dollars." She glanced at my check again and put the money back in the cash drawer.

Easily, I could have walked out the door with money that wasn't mine. Most of the time, temptation isn't really temptation, unless it's something desperately needed or wanted. I walked back to my car with the weight of a boulder in my chest. I *needed* ninety dollars.

Doing the right thing doesn't always make us feel good.

The repetitive dreams continued. I wondered why I kept having dreams about someone stealing my wallet or purse. Why can't we save any money?

I didn't get it. The struggle was real. I wouldn't spend money on myself because the kids and bills always came first. We rarely ate out. We sold our new car because we realized we could no longer afford the payment. Times were tight.

Search a dream dictionary for *"wallet"* and you'll find something like this:

> Your wallet symbolizes your self-identity or financial
> security.

To dream that your wallet has been stolen indicates that someone may be trying to take advantage of you. Perhaps someone has "stolen" your heart away. To dream that you lose your wallet suggests that you need to be more cautious and careful about your spending and finances. You need to be more responsible with your money.

To see an empty wallet in your dream represents financial worries. Alternatively, it refers to an emotional void or inner emptiness.

This definition almost hits the mark in *some* ways. Because we were struggling with money and because of the phrase *"someone has stolen your heart away."*

This is close to the **true** problem.

When we view this recurring dream about wallets spiritually instead, we discover the wallet dreams were about an issue with **my** heart. I was already extremely cautious with money and would hardly spend it. So, I didn't need to be more careful with spending. Yes, we did have financial worries during these dreams but also **testing** in real life.

God is sovereign. He taught me powerful lessons I could only grasp through real-life struggles. The dreams from God were about my spiritual growth, not literal finances. We were frugal with spending and saved as much as possible, but then, would have to spend it. It was almost as if God wouldn't allow us to have a supply of funds in the bank we could count on in hard times.

After many years, the final dream in the series of money dreams went something like this:

Someone stole my wallet or money from my wallet. I catch a glimpse of the thief and chase her until I finally catch up with her. I demanded my money back, and she handed it over. I reprimanded her for being

a thief and stealing my money. I really let her have it
verbally in the dream and vented a lot of steam.

I woke up. This time, I was amazed and shaken. I couldn't believe I got my wallet back and caught the thief. Plus, it felt good giving her a piece of my mind.

As I lay in bed contemplating the dream, a Scripture floated through my mind. The one about the love of money being the root of all evil.

> *For the love of money is a root of all kinds of evil.*
> *Some people, eager for money, have wandered from*
> *the faith and pierced themselves with many griefs. (1*
> *Timothy 6:10 NIV)*

Through the power of the Holy Spirit, I finally made the connection between the many stolen money dreams, our money issues in real life, and my mindset about money after I awoke from the final dream.

In my dream, the thief was some random woman, but I realized the true thief was *me*.

Stunned at this revelation, I was embarrassed; it took so long for me to see what God wanted me to understand. God had given me dream after dream, showing me truth, but I didn't get it. It took *many* dreams, Scripture, and seeking God's revelation through prayer before I finally recognized my sin.

- I loved money and the security it gave me sitting in a bank account.
- I didn't trust God regarding money.
- I didn't know money belonged to God.
- Money had become an idol.

Afterward, the dreams made perfect sense. Someone was taking something from me I *loved*. I felt violated because I believed it was *my* money. Truth is, nothing is really mine. God owns everything. Even money. I *trusted* having some money sitting in a bank account instead of trusting God. In essence, it was idolatry.

After this, I became acutely aware of God's ownership of all things, including money. He is our provider. He's not going to allow anyone or anything to take His place in our lives. I had a new mindset because God revealed my personal sin through dreams.

God's work in our dreams can change how we think.

We may not see it in our waking life, but He knows our lives will be better when we make the connection between God dreams and what the problem is in our waking life. There's an issue in our relationship with Him and He wants us to see the problem so our relationship will flourish.

This idolatry is something I have toted from childhood. The first time I received a legit paycheck at the tender age of thirteen, I loved having *my* own money. It became an idol because it gave me freedom to buy things I wanted. Before God began this work in me, it never crossed my mind that I trusted having money more than I trusted God.

I was **unaware** of my own sin.

I repented completely and released my hold on money in my life. I recognized it wasn't mine to save. It wasn't mine to spend. It wasn't mine, *period*. That's why I couldn't save it. God wasn't going to allow me to save until I understood who owned it. He wanted me to recognize He's my **provider**. He's going to take care of me no matter what.

I needed to stop trying to control money, stop *loving* it sitting in a bank account, and stop *trusting* it to get me through difficult times. I needed to trust God in every area of my life, and money was an area I was missing the mark. I didn't get it until He brought it to my attention through **recurring** dreams and life circumstances.

Truth:

Sin runs deep in our veins. We can hear someone tell us something is a sin, but until we "get it" on our own, we won't change. We may not even know we're sinning. We're so focused on our waking life; we don't pay attention to the sin God may be revealing through dreams.

Key:

Repetitive dreams often have spiritual significance. When God's purpose is recognized, the dreams will change us in our waking life.
The purposes of a person's heart are deep waters, but one who has insight draws them out. (Proverbs 20:5 NIV)

CHAPTER THREE

The Self-Examination Dream

As water reflects the face, so one's life reflects the heart. (Proverbs 27:19 NIV)

Gazing into a mirror in a dream, we might find a fault. Have you ever caught a glimpse of yourself in a mirror? Have you gazed intensely until you discovered something isn't right?

I've done this a few times as I've gone along my spiritual journey. I always find something that's not quite right. A bad spot on my tongue or a wiry hair growing out the side of my cheek. God is revealing an issue of the flesh.

Here is an example of a self-examination dream:

I was in the small bathroom of the little church I grew up in, examining myself in the mirror above the sink. I felt something on my tongue and stuck it out to see what was wrong. As I looked at my tongue, I noticed a bad spot with some flesh sticking out that shouldn't be there. I felt it until I could grasp the bad spot, then I began to pull it. I could feel my tongue unraveling as I pulled and pulled until my entire

tongue was gone all the way to the back of my throat.
I'd pulled out my entire tongue.

When I woke up, thankfully, my tongue was still there.

It doesn't take a lot of Scripture to know our tongues are often bad. It doesn't take much life to reveal the tongue's capabilities.

We start off life crying for everything we need and want. We let our wills be known by the time we're two years old, screaming "No!" to almost everything our parent wants us to do. We begin *lying* as soon as we realize it can get us out of trouble.

The tongue is a strong muscle and heals more quickly than any other muscle in the body. But oh, the damage those little muscles can cause when we use them in the wrong way.

> *Those who consider themselves religious and yet do not keep a tight rein on their tongues deceive themselves, and their religion is worthless. (James 1:26 NIV)*

> *Likewise, the tongue is a small part of the body, but it makes great boasts. Consider what a great forest is set on fire by a small spark. The tongue also is a fire, a world of evil among the parts of the body. It corrupts the whole body, sets the whole course of one's life on fire, and is itself set on fire by hell. All kinds of animals, birds, reptiles, and sea creatures are being tamed and have been tamed by mankind, but no human being can tame the tongue. It is a restless evil, full of deadly poison. With the tongue we praise our Lord and Father, and with it we curse human beings, who have been made in God's likeness. (James 3:5–9 NIV)*

At the time of the dream, I was in my early thirties, working at a claims processing center. I hated my job. There was only one man there. All the other employees were women. Sadly, some women gossip. I found myself in a situation at work where it seemed I'd get sucked into this type of behavior. But there were other life circumstances at the time that also made life difficult. I'm sure I complained a lot. We bought land to build a house near our family. But we were living in a tiny trailer on top of a hill with no washer and dryer because they were in storage. I had to go to the laundromat a couple of times a week and had two young sons at the time. My husband was driving a long distance to his job and didn't like his job either, to be honest. Complaints were common, unfortunately, at home and at work.

God won't put up with bad behavior from His children for long. He may give us opportunities to correct ourselves, but if we don't, He steps in. He is a master parent. He knows what it takes to stop bad behavior.

Here is one example of what happened at this workplace that helped me get a bit of control over my tongue.

I'd become good friends with several of the girls who worked with me. We were in a large training room, sitting close together in rows, at tables lined with computers, learning software. The girl next to me was funny, and we'd get cracked up a lot.

But on this day, a friend in front of us asked the teacher a question that had just been explained because she didn't get it. The funny girl next to me leaned over and said something derogatory just as the friend in front of me turned around and realized she was talking about her. I didn't say anything, but I also didn't defend my other friend. I didn't know what to do. It was obvious the friend in front of us was hurt by the behavior.

My heart sank. I wasn't even sure how to correct the situation. After rolling it around in my mind all night, the next day, I pulled the friend aside who had her feelings hurt and apologized. She completely understood and forgave me.

Sometimes, getting control of our tongue means making an apology when we didn't do anything wrong, but also didn't do what may have been right. God has high expectations regarding His other children.

Seeing why I pulled my tongue out in a dream is easy now that I'm older and wiser. God was showing me an area of my life that needed some major work. I needed to watch my words, my actions, and my reactions to others. This dream could also be filed under "sin revelation," but the dream was not repetitive; it was *jarring.* It got my attention, and I thought about it for years.

God may allow an embarrassing situation to expose our bad behavior. And He may give a jarring self-examination dream to get our attention to the offensive behavior.

If we look up the word *mirror* on a dream glossary website, we may find a definition like this:

> *To dream of your own reflection in the mirror suggests that you are pondering thoughts about your inner self. The reflection in the mirror is how you perceive yourself or how you want others to see you. You may be contemplating strengthening and changing aspects of your character. To see a mirror in your dream symbolizes a loved one or good friend. Dreaming about a mirror is also symbolic of the truth.*

Now, this definition is helpful, I admit. We are reflecting on our true selves when we see ourselves in a mirror. It is symbolic of truth. But we need to consider this dream in a spiritual way.

I did **not** think I had a problem with my tongue until God brought it to my attention.

The fault we see is something representing a problem we struggle with in our flesh, and it needs to be corrected.

Truth:

God is showing us an area of our flesh that needs to be cut off as we move along our Christian journey. Unfortunately, we may struggle with some areas of our flesh until our bodies physically die and we are rid of the sin nature.

Key:

Recognize the self-examination dream as God showing us something's not quite right in our spiritual walk. Eventually, the dream will affect our waking lives. God is at work changing us from the inside out and making us humble.

May these words of my mouth and this meditation of my heart be pleasing in your sight, LORD, my Rock and my Redeemer. (Psalm 19:14 NIV)

Part Two

The Soul

CHAPTER FOUR

God *Literally* Speaks in Dreams

G od has spoken to people through dreams many times in the Bible. He's direct. He's not using pictures or riddles. He is using words. He's giving directions. He's giving a warning. He's giving instructions.

Below are examples:

> Then God came to Laban the Aramean in a dream at night and said to him, "Be careful not to say anything to Jacob, either good or bad." (Genesis 31:24 NIV)

> At Gibeon the LORD appeared to Solomon during the night in a dream, and God said, "Ask for whatever you want me to give you." Solomon answered, "You have shown great kindness to your servant, my father David, because he was faithful to you and righteous and upright in heart. You have continued this great kindness to him and have given him a son to sit on his throne this very day. "Now, LORD my God, you have made your servant king in place of my father David. But I am only a little child and do not know how to carry out my duties. Your servant is here

among the people you have chosen, a great people, too numerous to count or number. So, give your servant a discerning heart to govern your people and to distinguish between right and wrong. For who is able to govern this great people of yours?" The Lord was pleased that Solomon had asked for this. So God said to him, "Since you have asked for this and not for long life or wealth for yourself, nor have asked for the death of your enemies but for discernment in administering justice, I will do what you have asked. I will give you a wise and discerning heart, so that there will never have been anyone like you, nor will there ever be. Moreover, I will give you what you have not asked for—both wealth and honor—so that in your lifetime you will have no equal among kings. And if you walk in obedience to me and keep my decrees and commands as David your father did, I will give you a long life." Then Solomon awoke—and he realized it had been a dream. (1 Kings 3:5–15 NIV)

God doesn't change. He does the same thing today. I've experienced this type of dream a few times. A direct question or statement. One of those dreams was about death. My death. I was asked the following question in a short dream.

Here is the dream:

"How would you feel if you died?"
I thought for a moment and answered, "I'd be happy to see Jesus."

I woke up and thought my answer was true. That is how I'd feel if I died. God worked while I slept getting my "real" answer—my heart.

I think He liked my answer because He set me free from something hindering me in many ways. An area of my life Satan had his grubby little hands on. I didn't want to cross big bridges. I was afraid to fly. I'd get a pang in my stomach at the thought of physically passing away. Funerals gave me the creeps.

What ultimately happened because of this dream (in my waking life) is God set me free from a bondage many are in—the fear of death. Not long after this short dream where I was asked a question about death, I began to have repetitive dreams about my death. There were many dreams for a couple of years. I wondered about them but never considered God may be at work in my dreams. I didn't yet have the awareness of such things.

Here is one of those dreams:

> *I was bitten by a black mamba and was terror-stricken because I knew I would not survive. I was on a beach in a foreign country and told an older lady there with me, "I think I'm going to die." She only nodded with a look of great concern on her face for my well-being. I didn't understand why she didn't help me.*

I awoke horrified, but relieved it was a dream.

In my waking life, God was also working. I had some heart issues and a minor cancer scare. These were intertwined with the dreams for a couple of years. Eventually, the series of death dreams led to the final dream where I awoke and recognized my fear was gone.

Here is the dream:

> *I was asleep but woke up and sat up in bed. Something didn't feel quite right. I felt my head, and it felt hard and numb. I couldn't feel anything. It didn't even feel like my own head. Then my body fell away from me,*

back onto the bed in an awkward position. I was left sitting up. I could see my body lying in the bed . . . dead.

I was out of my body and free. It felt incredible. I became completely giddy. There was no way you could have talked me into getting back inside that body.

Then I heard loud wailing, but not like someone crying at a funeral. It had an odd tone. I perceived the sound was coming from demons wailing in grief because they lost their power over me and were going back to hell.

I woke up.

As with many other dreams in my life, I still felt what I'd experienced in the dream. Free and giddy. When I told a Christian friend about the dream, she immediately brought my attention to a Scripture in Hebrews:

Since the children have flesh and blood, he too shared in their humanity so that by his death he might break the power of him who holds the power of death—that is, the devil—and free those who all their lives were held in slavery by their fear of death. For surely it is not angels he helps, but Abraham's descendants. (Hebrews 2:14–16 NIV)

Confirmation from a friend affirming God's work in my life while I slept. I didn't even think to look to Scripture because I wasn't aware of how powerfully He was working in my life.

Some might have thought this dream was not from God because there was demonic activity in the dream. But I digress. God can show us whatever He wants in a dream, including demonic activity. But the dream is from God.

Why would Satan show us a dream revealing our freedom and demons going back to hell? He likes to keep such things hidden. God is the One who reveals truth and the One who sets His children free.

We read where Elihu (Job's young friend) states in his speech to Job:

> *For God does speak—now one way—now another,*
> *though no one perceives it. (Job 33:14 NIV)*

Could it be that God is speaking, and we don't recognize His voice because it comes in a way we don't expect? Could it be we don't *perceive* it?

My life changed dramatically due to this series of dreams God gave, revealing bondage. I was still growing up spiritually and had absolutely no idea. But He knew. He saw His child trapped in a snare of the devil. He set me free to enjoy life to its fullest without fearing death.

Through the final dream, He gave me a glimpse of how it feels to be free of our flesh. I experienced freedom and never wanted to go back. He also showed me how much Satan doesn't want us free. Satan entangles us with issues of our flesh to control us and inhibit us from fulfilling our full potential on Earth as we serve God. He doesn't want us to live an abundant life in Christ.

I no longer fear crossing a bridge. I no longer get a pang in my stomach at the thought of physical death. I'm no longer afraid to fly. Funerals are no longer a problem.

I'm free.

Truth:

God may ask a question in a dream to get to the heart of the matter. Then He begins a work in us that reflects His character and changes our lives. This is spiritual transformation.

Key:

The result of a series of dreams will reflect God's character. Here he set His child free from a spiritual bondage in real life.

I will walk about in freedom, for I have sought out your precepts. (Psalm 119:45 NIV)

CHAPTER FIVE

A Prophetic Dream

A thousand years in your sight are like a day that has just gone by, or like a watch in the night. (Psalm 90:4 NIV)

Prophetic dreams are somewhat common for me these days. God gives me a heads-up and it thrills me to receive such a gift. These dreams sometimes startle me or make me wonder about them for days. I'm *never* able to guess their meaning until reality happens. Though sometimes, I'm on guard because I know something is going to happen. I'm only able to interpret the meaning after the life event. *Then* it is as clear as water drawn from a well.

Here is one of my favorite prophetic dreams regarding Joseph. He has a dream in his youth which comes true when he's an adult, twenty-two years later. It is one of many prophetic dreams mentioned in the Bible.

Joseph had a dream, and when he told it to his brothers, they hated him all the more. He said to them, "Listen to this dream I had: We were binding sheaves of grain out in the field when suddenly my sheaf rose and stood upright, while your sheaves gathered around mine and bowed down to it."

His brothers said to him, "Do you intend to reign over us? Will you actually rule us?" And they hated him all the more because of his dream and what he had said.

Then he had another dream, and he told it to his brothers. "Listen," he said, "I had another dream, and this time the sun and moon and the eleven stars were bowing down to me."

When he told his father as well as his brothers, his father rebuked him and said, "What is this dream you had? Will your mother and I and your brothers actually come and bow down to the ground before you?" His brothers were jealous of him, but his father kept the matter in mind. (Genesis 37:5–11 NIV)

To be honest, it shocked me that Jacob knew the meaning of Joseph's dream right away. And he was right. (Because this ability completely eludes me.) Another thing to notice is that God gave Joseph two dreams in a row, about the same thing, in different ways. Something **important** to remember.

Later, Joseph is sold into slavery by his jealous brothers. He goes to jail and eventually becomes the governor and second in command of Egypt because he deciphered the meaning of Pharaoh's disturbing dreams, foretelling seven years of abundance and then seven years of famine. When Pharaoh tells Joseph about his dreams so that he can interpret them, Joseph says the **important** thing to remember in Genesis 41.

Then Joseph said to Pharaoh, "The dreams of Pharaoh are one and the same. God has revealed to Pharaoh what he is about to do. (Genesis 41:25 NIV)

The reason the dream was given to Pharaoh in two forms is that the matter has been firmly decided by God, and God will do it soon." (Genesis 41:32 NIV)

Interesting concept for us to remember when we're analyzing our own dreams.

But back to Joseph.

His brothers end up coming to him, unaware he's their younger brother they sold into slavery years earlier. Pharaoh has placed him in a position of power, distributing the grains they've stored because of the famine. His brothers do indeed humbly come to Joseph and bow down before him just as he dreamed in his youth. Joseph's prophetic dream became reality twenty-two years later.

We know that Joseph told his brothers about the **two** dreams when he had them, and they were prophetic. Pharaoh told Joseph about his **two** prophetic dreams. We may also find ourselves having **two** similar dreams about the same thing, and they are both from God telling us in advance about something that has been firmly decided, and He will do it soon.

For me, these types of dreams usually stun me. I'm floored when the reality happens, and I know God cared enough to show me what was going to happen in advance.

Here's an example of a recent prophetic dream of mine (italics is all dream):

I was somewhere in the country in a large barn and I couldn't find a way out. I noticed a man I know walking toward the barn. I was desperately trying to flee before he got there because I did not want to talk to this man. But I'm unable to escape.

I woke up.

How *strange*. Why am I dreaming about a man I no longer speak to, and haven't in years? We had a major falling out many years ago, and the whole incident caused my family to leave our church. It was a heartbreaking situation.

But after I woke up and got busy with my workday, I quickly forgot the dream and didn't give it much thought. Then a few nights later, I had another dream that involved this same person.

Here is the dream:

I'm standing in line for some sort of event with this man I no longer speak to. We're both dressed up, and he is wearing a suit. I'm wearing a sparkly silver dress. We're entering some nice place, waiting for someone to acknowledge our presence. Then we're inside, and it seems like a prom or something like that to me. We see a place where we can have our photo taken and so we go to have a picture together. There's a cranky lady there who oversees the camera. The camera is down on the floor, and we can't see ourselves. So, I ask her, "Can you please raise the camera so we can see what we look like?"

She rolls her eyes at me like it is a lot of trouble, but she reluctantly lifts the camera, and we see ourselves and start smiling and taking "selfies" somehow. We're laughing and having a great time, and right as the last photo clicked, I raise my right hand in a peace symbol, but it's too late, and our photo session is over. I said, "Aw, we should have done this!" as I'm raising my hand again in a peace sign. But we just laughed some more and moved on from the camera station. Then it's time to leave. I see him from the backside as I'm leaving, like I'm looking back at him, and see him standing there facing away from me wearing his suit.

I woke up. The dream fresh in my mind, I revisited it in confusion. Why am I dressed up like I'm on a date with this person? Why were we laughing and having a good time like we were dating or, at least, *friends*? Bizarre. I thought about the dream for a few days, then it left my mind. I honestly thought maybe it had to do with writing for some strange reason.

Then, before long, it's Valentine's Day. My husband had bought tickets to an event, and we were excited to go. He spent a lot of money on our date. The table was close to the stage and included a nice dinner, dessert, and live entertainment. The package he purchased included roses on the table for me and a small package of chocolates and such.

We dressed nicely and headed out for our Valentine's date. We arrived at the venue, which was a large, fancy barn where many weddings and events are held. We stood in line waiting for the host to lead us to our seats. We found our table, and the food buffet was open, so we were advised to go ahead and get a plate of food. The desserts were set out on each table, and I could already tell mine would be scrumptious. It was white cake with coconut frosting, one of my favorites.

We filled our plates with delicious food as the room filled with more and more people. We sat down at our assigned table and began eating our meal. The tables were set for six to eight guests, and soon others joined us. A sharp-dressed lady sat down across from us. At first, I was concerned because, immediately, she began complaining about everything. "Oh, my roses are wilted." She held the roses and sniffed them. Then, after she sat down and noticed the dessert waiting for her, she added, "This cake is *dry*."

I thought it was going to be a lovely evening listening to all this negativity. But eventually, her husband joined her, and we began conversing with them and enjoyed their company.

It wasn't long before we decided to take some selfies at our fancy Valentine's dinner. My husband and I smiled and snapped photos. During our smiling and photo snapping, someone came up behind us and put his arms on our shoulders and photo-bombed one of our selfies. We laughed, not even knowing who it was, and kept snapping photos. When we were done, we viewed the photos a few seconds later and realized the person bombing our photo was someone we used to go to church with. The church where our hearts were broken over ten years earlier.

When we realized who the photobomber was, we looked for him in the room and noticed he was sitting behind us at a different table not far away. Then we saw the person sitting across from him and it was the man we no longer speak to, for the most part, and his wife.

A bit of a bummer, if I'm honest. After the initial shock, we settled into conversing with others at our table. The sharp-dressed lady who complained a lot asked me if I'd take a photo of her and her husband, then handed me her phone. I snapped some pictures from up high as a courtesy to put them in the best angle.

Then she offered to take one of us. So, I handed her my phone, and she held it down low, almost to the table, to take the photos. Vain as it may be, I prefer to have photos taken from higher than my face, so I asked her, "Can you please raise the camera up so we will look thinner?" I laughed. Then immediately remembered asking a similar question in a dream. *Can you please raise the camera so we can see what we look like?*

The reality of what was happening almost buckled my knees. I was dressed up (not as fancy as the dream though) and on a date, and the man in my dream (that I no longer speak with) was also dressed up and on a date. We were not on a date together, but in the *same place*.

The dream had been prophetic. The reality was playing out as I realized it. Detail after detail began coming to mind from the dream that matched reality. It was blowing my mind for the rest of the night. We stood in line to go in, and it was fancy. The cranky lady in the dream raising the camera and the complaining lady sitting across from me at the table taking our photo and me asking her to raise the camera.

The dream had also been given to me two times. The first dream was me trying to get out of a large barn and seeing the man coming with me finding no escape. The second dream was a fun sort of dream, even though it caught me off guard. God gave me the dream in a way that made me remember it, for sure. It made me think I was on a date with this man that I don't even speak to in life. So, it was sort of shocking, and I remembered every detail.

It's ironic that I wanted to throw up the "peace" sign in the dream, but we were too late. Maybe this is God orchestrating a peace treaty between us.

So, this is the perfect example of a prophetic dream given two times and the reality that followed. Something to consider as you begin a journey of examining dreams and seeking God in them.

And the experience of recognizing the dream as reality unfolded is *key* as you'll read in the next chapter.

Truth:

> *God is all-knowing. We are "in" time while on earth. He is not. Past, present, and future are all before Him at the same time. He proves Himself to His children by giving dreams that show life events in advance.*

Key:

Prophetic dreams draw us into a deeper relationship with God. They draw us to worship an all-knowing God who sees everything and cares enough to give us a heads-up.

Joseph had a dream, and when he told it to his brothers, they hated him all the more. (Genesis 37:5 NIV)

CHAPTER SIX

Déjà Vu
(Already Seen)

But do not forget this one thing, dear friends: With the Lord, a day is like a thousand years, and a thousand years is like a day. (2 Peter 3:8 NIV)

Have you ever experienced déjà vu?

A good definition found online is this:

"Déjà Vu" is a common intuitive experience that has happened to many of us. The expression is derived from the French, meaning "already seen." When it occurs, it seems to spark our memory of a place we've already been, a person we've already seen, or an act we have already done.

You understand the weirdness of it all if you've had déjà vu. A surreal feeling comes over us. *I've been to this place before. I've met this person already. I've already done this.* But it wasn't in real life—or in a *previous* life, as some may suggest—it was in a dream.

Déjà vu is an *unrecognized* prophetic dream coming to fruition.

Because we don't remember or make dream connections yet (because we've not learned to do so), we don't realize what is happening at that moment. Instead of being in the place before or meeting the person previously, etc.—you were given the events in advance in a dream but don't remember the dream or make the connection to the dream when the *reality* happens.

How do I know this?

Because I used to have déjà vu **often**. Now, it's rare.

Instead, I'm stunned because I vividly remember the dream as it forces its way into reality right before my eyes.

How did I get to the place where I recognize what used to be the surreal experience of déjà vu to recognizing a dream I had sometime previously *become* reality?

Interestingly, not on purpose.

The difference between experiencing déjà vu and recognizing it as a dream is through the power of the indwelling Holy Spirit. He can bring to our minds the dream we had—reminding us of His work while we slept. But we must be in tune with how God is speaking to us.

When I began making this connection was after a *total sur-render* to God.

It all started in the fall of 1993 with a frightening dream when I was twenty-four years old.

Here is the dream:

> I was led into a graveyard by a Grim Reaper-type of spirit who pointed me toward a specific fresh grave. I knew it was my child. I began to grieve and begged the spirit, "Please, let me hold him. Please, let me hold him one more time!" He nodded, and suddenly my child was in my arms. I held him close and squeezed him tight, grieving deeply. Then, this beautiful energy began flowing from my heart to the heart of my child. Back and forth, back and forth, until I finally let go.

I woke up horrified. I only had one son, and he was four years old at the time. I worked at his daycare and told my coworkers about the terrible dream. I was advised this was a dream from the devil using my fears against me.

That had never even crossed my mind. But at this time, I knew nothing of God working in dreams in my life and, to be honest, I didn't even know Him that well. But I pondered the words of wisdom from the older daycare worker. Her husband had been a popular Christian singer, and she seemed confident in her answer.

But would a dream influenced by Satan show me the death of my own son, and allow me to hold him and feel that beautiful energy? I was confused as I contemplated the dream. As the weeks passed, the dream slipped into my memory, and I moved on with my life.

Then, surprisingly, I discovered I was pregnant a few weeks later. I'd been pregnant at the time of the dream but didn't know it yet. We were excited even though the child wasn't planned. We couldn't even wait to tell people and began informing family and friends of the little bundle of joy coming our way.

Shortly after announcing our exciting baby news, I woke up in the middle of the night in pain, cramping. I went back to sleep and didn't give it any thought. I woke up the next morning and discovered I'd miscarried.

Anyone who has lost a baby they already love can understand the despair that hit my heart. I was crushed. Then, I became angry. Why would God allow this?

Then my husband made it worse by suggesting that maybe it was for the best.

In his defense, we were young, and he was pursuing a music career. But his response to my devastation fueled my anger. I couldn't even bring myself to talk to him for two weeks. I wouldn't talk to God either, even though I kept feeling Him calling me to pray. I would not do it. If I haven't mentioned it yet, I was spiritually immature at this time, like a toddler having a little fit in God's presence. I was holding my breath in a tantrum, refusing to breathe while my face turned purple.

One night, at the end of the two weeks, I was at my breaking point. Everyone in the house was asleep while I folded a basket of laundry in the living room. As I got up to head to bed, I felt God calling me to pray again. I refused. Then, before I reached the bedroom, I felt Him calling me to pray again and, in my desperation, said in my spirit, "What do you want from me?"

"Get on your knees." The authoritative answer came quickly to my spirit.

I walked into my bedroom and hit my knees beside the bed while my husband snoozed on the other side.

Immediately, on my knees, I was swept into an incredible silent prayer as tears streamed down my face. An energy flowed through me, and it felt like a hug from heaven. The energy continued as I prayed words I never intended to pray and saw things as God saw them. I was selfish. Five minutes before this, I never would have thought that. But there it was. I used the word "*surrender*" in my prayer, which is not something I ever heard in the little church I grew up in. I promised I'd go to Him first with everything in my life going forward. This was a powerful, life-changing prayer.

The experience is longer and more detailed than I'm recording here because I just want to record how the surreal experiences went from déjà vu to jaw-dropping remembrance of a dream.

(A side note: Back to the dream about the Grim Reaper showing me a fresh grave that was my child. Now, it is clear God was giving me a prophetic dream about the death of a child I was unaware I was carrying at the time of the dream. He even allowed me to hold the baby and experience the love of a child I'd never get to hold. This *blows* my mind. I never made this connection until many years later when I began to understand how God was working in my dreams.)

Before this surrender beside my bed, déjà vu would get my attention, and I'd wonder, "Why do I feel like I've been here before? Why does it seem like I've met this person before? What is going on?"

After this surrender beside my bed, my life changed in a powerful way.

Shortly after the surrender, I began to recognize those moments of déjà vu as a dream I'd had earlier. Sometimes, a few days earlier. Sometimes, a few weeks earlier. When I began making this connection, the surreal feeling stopped, and I recognized God had shown it to me in a dream.

Waking up from terrifying, **dramatized** dreams with my heart pounding also became common during this time. Those dreams, where I awoke in a panic with a vivid dream running through my mind, became a clue to realize it was a dream from God. Though they were most often over-the-top dramatized, the reality was never as bad as the dream. This gave me another clue. God was getting my attention with "dream drama" so I'd remember them because they were important. He was speaking to me in a *new* way, and He wanted me to make that connection.

I know this is an uncommon experience. At least, it appears to be uncommon, as I've gone through my Christian life. I've met a few Christians who speak of extraordinary experiences with God, but not too many people seem to have them. But God deals with His children on an individual basis, and we are not all the same.

I'm a dreamer, that much I know. God made me this way. I didn't try to make myself have déjà vu, and I didn't try to start having dreams with reality checks. God did it. I don't know why. I have no control over when I have a dream or why God chooses to speak to me through a dream. It's His gift to me because He's a giver. And I think He loves shaking things up in my life and stunning me with His ability to show me whatever He chooses. I'm always in awe when I recognize the reality of a dream.

If you have déjà vu, you're a dreamer—you just aren't making the connection. If you are a dreamer but haven't surrendered to God and been possessed by the indwelling Holy Spirit, you will continue to have déjà vu because God is the one who reveals the meaning of dreams. God within us is the connector between dreams and reality.

> *"This is the dream that I, King Nebuchadnezzar had. Now, Belteshazzar, tell me what it means, because none of the wise men in my kingdom can interpret it for me. But you can because the spirit of the holy gods is in you." (Daniel 4:18 NIV)*

In the previous chapter is a good example of recognizing a dream instead of having the strange feeling of déjà vu. The exact moment I recognized the dream was when I asked the lady across the table to raise the camera. Before God began revealing the **exact dream** to me, I would have just been overwhelmed with the strange, surreal feeling instead of recognizing a prophetic dream. I never would have made the connection, and I would've spent the entire time thinking I'd been there before. I'd have thought, "I've met this lady across the table before."

But instead, because of my relationship with God and with the indwelling Holy Spirit working powerfully in my life, I *now* recognize the exact dream. It is mind-blowing to have this experience, and I hope I never take it for granted.

Truth:

> *The word* déjà vu *isn't in the Bible.*
> *But what* déjà vu **actually is**—*is found in the Bible. It's a prophetic dream (unrecognized by the dreamer) coming to reality. Ask God to help you make this*

connection through the power of the Holy Spirit and see God at work while you sleep.

Key:

Prophetic dreams draw us into a deeper relationship with God. They're proof He is at work in our life. Daniel replied, "No wise man, enchanter, magician or diviner can explain to the king the mystery he has asked about, but there is a God in heaven who reveals mysteries.
(Daniel 2:27–28a NIV)

CHAPTER SEVEN

God Answers Prayer with a Dream

ave you ever prayed fervently about a situation but felt God never answered?

We can feel frustrated by an unanswered prayer. We can even grow angry if we're desperate for an answer to a troubling situation in our lives. We may question God's love for us.

If God loves me, why doesn't He give me an answer?

Sometimes the reason we don't hear from God is simple. The answer is **no**. Sometimes, He's cultivating patience and He's asking us to wait until the time is right. But one thing I learned in my study of dreams is, sometimes, God answers our inquiries with a dream.

I already wondered if this was possible, because in 2014 I'd prayed for truth about a life situation and God gave me a vivid dream with detailed symbolism. I believed it was my answer, but I never really studied it to have biblical backup.

So, if you feel God isn't answering, consider that *maybe* He did—in a dream. You just never made the connection of God's work while you slept.

He inquired of the LORD, but the LORD did not an-
swer him by dreams or Urim or prophets. (1 Samuel
28:6 NIV)

In the Scripture reference found in 1 Samuel, we see Saul has inquired of the Lord, but God didn't answer him. One of the ways God *didn't* answer Saul was by **dreams**.

Honestly, when I read that Scripture, I stopped in my tracks. I read it over and over and let it sink in. God *answers* us with dreams, or the Bible wouldn't have Scripture stating He didn't answer Saul in this way. It would *not* be there. Saul expected an answer to his inquiry in one of those three ways.

Just to give some perspective on the Scripture, Saul is desperate for help because the Philistines are closing in on him. Yet, God doesn't answer him. Saul becomes so desperate that he puts on a disguise and asks a medium to bring Samuel back from the dead for help. (Bad idea by the way!)

We may become so desperate for an answer from God that we do something silly, too. Like question His love for us.

So, we must consider all the ways God answers our pleas. Dreams are one way He might be answering. We don't make a connection because we've never thought of dreams in such a way. Or, maybe, like many other people, we don't pay attention to our dreams.

Another Scripture where the answer to prayer is given through a dream (or night vision) is found in Daniel 2:17–23. Daniel is distressed due to King Nebuchadnezzar's mandate that the wise men of Babylon (which included Daniel and his friends) not only tell him the meaning of a disturbing dream he had, but also that they tell him the **content** of the dream.

They will all be executed if they're unable to give him the details of the dream along with the meaning. Of course, Daniel, in all his wisdom, turns to God for help.

Then Daniel returned to his house and explained the matter to his friends Hananiah, Mishael and Azariah. He urged them to plead for mercy from the God of heaven concerning this mystery, so that he and his friends might not be executed with the rest of the wise men of Babylon. During the night the mystery was revealed to Daniel in a vision. Then Daniel praised the God of heaven. (Daniel 2:17–19 NIV)

Amazing.

God may be answering many of our prayers or inquiries in this way. Of course, we love it when He answers in an easier way for us to understand. But as mentioned in Job 33:

For God does speak—now one way—now another, though no one perceives it.

In a dream, in a vision of the night, when deep sleep falls on people as they slumber in their beds, he may speak in their ears and terrify them with warnings, to turn them away from their wrongdoing and keep them from pride, to preserve them from the pit, their lives from perishing from the sword. (Job 33:14–18 NIV)

If we begin to ask God to show us in a dream, He just may.

I won't give the personal details of my inquiry of the Lord where He answered me vividly with a symbolic dream. But I asked God to tell me the *truth* about a situation, and He did.

Just not in the way I expected.

We do need to have discernment in this area with dreams, and it may be necessary to be spiritually mature to make the distinction of an answered prayer in this way. God does speak often in symbols, which can be difficult for us to understand. A puzzle to solve.

What we may see as literal meaning may be spiritual meaning. We ponder the dream in this way without taking it literally. (Though I would never rule out the literal meaning.)

Truth:

> God answers our desperate pleas in many ways. Sometimes, He speaks clearly to our spirit while we're awake. Sometimes, He speaks through the Bible or another Christian. Sometimes, He speaks in a dream or a night vision.

Key:

> Know that a vivid dream could be God answering our inquiry or prayer. God is at work while we sleep: speaking to us, changing us, and revealing truth.
> Praise be to God, who has not rejected my prayer or withheld his love from me!
> (Psalm 66:20 NIV)

CHAPTER EIGHT

Symbolism in Our Sleep

When Jacob awoke from his sleep, he thought, "Surely the LORD is in this place, and I was not aware of it."
(Genesis 28:16 NIV)

I love the Bible.
I love Scripture.
I love how God speaks.

Anytime we desire, we can open the Bible and read about what God has done. He can speak intimately through His Word. But how interesting it is He'd choose to speak to us in a dream with symbolism.

One of my favorite symbolic dreams is found in Genesis.

> *Jacob left Beersheba and set out for Harran. When he reached a certain place, he stopped for the night because the sun had set. Taking one of the stones there, he put it under his head and lay down to sleep. He had a dream in which he saw a stairway resting on the earth, with its top reaching to heaven, and the angels of God were ascending and descending on it. There above it stood the LORD, and he said: "I*

am the LORD, the God of your father Abraham and the God of Isaac. I will give you and your descendants the land on which you are lying. Your descendants will be like the dust of the earth, and you will spread out to the west and to the east, to the north and to the south. All peoples on earth will be blessed through you and your offspring. I am with you and will watch over you wherever you go, and I will bring you back to this land. I will not leave you until I have done what I promised you."

When Jacob awoke from his sleep, he thought, "Surely the LORD is in this place, and I was not aware of it." He was afraid and said, "How awesome is this place! This is none other than the house of God; this is the gate of heaven."

Early the next morning Jacob took the stone he had placed under his head and set it up as a pillar and poured oil on top of it. He called that place Bethel, though the city used to be called Luz. Then Jacob made a vow, saying, "If God will be with me and will watch over me on this journey I am taking and will give me food to eat and clothes to wear so that I return safely to my father's household, then the LORD will be my God and this stone that I have set up as a pillar will be God's house, and of all that you give me I will give you a tenth." (Genesis 18:10–22 NIV)

The dream given to Jacob was symbolic and prophetic. We know God kept His promise. Jacob did return to his father's household. We also know *all peoples have been blessed* through Jacob because Jacob became Israel. His children were the children of Israel. Jesus came from the tribe of Judah, who was one of the sons of Jacob (or Israel).

God speaks truth in dreams and keeps His promises.

I've had the coolest symbolic dreams. Literally. When I have an awesome symbolic dream, I wake up and am like, "Top ten dream!"

Here is one of those dreams:

> *The wind stirred sticks and leaves into the air as I stood in the grocery store parking lot. A storm was brewing. I saw a girl I knew from high school coming out of a clothing store nearby. She loved shopping and didn't care what she bought. She just wanted to spend money.*
>
> *I turned from her and closed my eyes as the wind rushed all around me. I decided I wanted to fly. I opened my eyes, ran as fast as I could, and jumped into the wind. It picked me up and took me higher and higher until I was floating above the town. Relaxed and at peace with nothing holding me up but air, I rolled over onto my back and rested my arms across my chest. I floated effortlessly, carried by the wind. It took me west of town, closer to the home I grew up in.*

I woke up on my back with my arms resting across my chest, just like in the dream. The same peaceful feeling lingered in my spirit. I pondered the details of the incredible dream before falling back to sleep.

What an amazing symbolic dream! I thought about it for weeks. Obviously, I still think about it.

Why was I at a shopping mall? Why was I in the town where I grew up? Why did I want to jump up into the wind? Why did the wind hold me up and carry me around town and then toward my childhood home out Highway 8 West? Why did I wake up in the same physical position I was in when I was being carried by the wind in my dream?

What I do know is that the person who just wanted to spend money could be me or a ton of other people. It's a sin we may not recognize in our waking life. The wind represents the Holy Spirit. My willingness to jump into it and allow it to hold me up and carry me around without being afraid of falling is reflecting my faith and trust in God to carry me wherever He chooses.

This dream was one of many given during the repetitive money dreams I had, revealing my sin regarding money mentioned in Chapter Two, where God worked in my sleep, showing me the error of my ways through sin revelation.

Dreams of this nature cause us to think about the meaning and God's intent in giving these to us. Thinking on them over and over again and seeing the meaning over time draws us deeper in our relationship with God. This is one reason why He'd give such an incredible dream. There's nothing quite like waking from a dream like this and pondering the meaning—knowing it's a gift from God.

Another more recent symbolic dream is one I think of often, and I am slowly seeing the meaning, making its purpose known.

Here is the dream I had in March 2016:

> *I was standing on the ground, in front of the little church I grew up in, where my dad was the pastor, and I spent many Sunday mornings in worship. I was looking to my left at the church where my husband was standing on the porch, staring at me with fear on his face and reaching for me. That's when I turned my gaze straight ahead, and in front of me, I saw a lion slowly walking toward me.*

For a split second, fear rose, but as soon as I made eye contact with the lion, the fear disappeared, and I knew the lion wasn't there to harm me, and I trusted God that he wouldn't.

The lion walked between the church building and where I was standing on the ground and lay down next to me. (Between me and the church and my husband) I then looked at my husband with fear still in his eyes and turned away from him and lay down next to the lion on the ground. The lion was behind me, and I was lying on my right side facing the road. There was something big in front of me, and I thought it could be a bigger wild animal, but I really don't know. There was a great shadow there blocking my view. But I never felt more protected and safer in my entire life, lying on the ground with a lion behind me and a great shadow before me. I was sandwiched between the two.

I woke up.

I truly believe Jesus was taking His rightful place in my life. He was stepping between me and the little church I loved so much from my youth—along with my husband, whom I also loved from my youth. I trusted God enough to turn away from both of those things and turn my back on them, trusting the lion wasn't going to harm me but was protecting me by lying down between me and those two loves of mine.

Then, in front of me there was some great unknown, but I felt safe and protected. Ready to face whatever lies ahead, knowing Jesus has my back.

Whoever dwells in the shelter of the Most High will rest in the shadow of the Almighty. (Psalm 91:1 NIV)

This Scripture comes to mind when I ponder this dream. I chose to lie down next to the lion and dwell in His shelter, and I never felt more protected. Before me was a great shadow, so I could have been resting in the shadow of the Almighty—literally.

If we search for the word *lion* on a website for dream symbols, we'd find this type of definition:

To see a lion in your dreams symbolizes great strength, courage, aggression, and power. You will overcome some of your emotional difficulties. As king of the jungle, the lion also represents dignity, royalty, leadership, pride, and domination. You have much influence over others. You also need to exercise some restraint in your own personal and social life.

The lion does represent great strength, royalty, and power. But it is not us, the lion represented Jesus in my dream. I lay on the ground beside him, and this represented my grounding in Christ. But this took a while for me to recognize—in fact, years.

See how this could be difficult to analyze a God dream using a glossary for dreams? We must allow God to give us the interpretation through the power of the Holy Spirit. It could be helpful to search an online Bible to get a better understanding of what the symbol God is using in the dream may mean.

Still, the interpretation is most likely personal.

Truth:

God speaks with symbolism. When we're able to make the connection between a dream symbol used by God and what He's telling us, we are amazed He'd speak to us in such a way.

Key:

Symbolic dreams intrigue us. This type of dream keeps our minds on God for a long time as we ponder the meaning, which also draws us to worship God. (Jacob anointed the pillar where he had the dream as an act of worship.)

Trust in the LORD and do good; dwell in the land and enjoy safe pasture. (Psalm 37:3 NIV)

Part Three

The Mind

CHAPTER NINE

CHAPTER NINE

All Your Mind

*"Teacher, which is the greatest commandment in the Law?" Jesus replied: "'Love the Lord your God with all your **heart** and with all your **soul** and with all your **mind**.' This is the first and greatest commandment. And the second is like it: 'Love your neighbor as yourself.' All the Law and the Prophets hang on these two commandments." (Matthew 22:36–40 NIV)*

What does this Scripture found in Matthew have to do with our dreams?

EVERYTHING.

It has to do with our minds.

While we sleep, our nature comes to life within some of our dreams. Our sin is not hidden because we're unconscious. We're unable to stop ourselves from doing things we'd never do willingly while awake. In some dreams, we may commit murder, adultery, or any manner of behavior we find appalling while conscious. However, God is showing us our sinful nature in our dreams. He may show us the sinful nature of others. He might test our hearts, souls, and minds while we sleep.

We'd never kill someone intentionally, and we wouldn't commit adultery. But we fall asleep and find ourselves in those exact situations. We may commit dreadful sins while we sleep.

Why?

To humble us.

There's not a direct example of God testing us in our dreams that I could find in the Bible. However, in Deuteronomy, God warns about prophets or dreamers who try to get His children to follow **other** gods.

> *If a prophet, or one who foretells by dreams, appears among you and announces to you a sign or wonder, and if the sign or wonder spoken of takes place, and the prophet says, "let us follow other gods" (gods you have not known) "and let us worship them," you must not listen to the words of that prophet or dreamer. The Lord your God is testing you to find out whether you love him with all your heart and with all your soul. It is the Lord your God you must follow, and him you must revere. Keep his commands and obey him; serve him and hold fast to him. (Deuteronomy 13:1–4 NIV)*

So, God does test us and dreams are involved. A dream from God **will** draw us deeper in relationship with Him—not some other god or idol.

We must be careful when sharing our dreams and interpreting them. I can't begin to express how long it took me to realize God was working in my dreams to *change* **me**. It was so difficult because dreams are so wild sometimes and hard to understand. To be honest, I can't interpret a dream until after reality makes me remember. I'd be terrible at foretelling the future based on a dream. Yes, many of my dreams are prophetic, and I may perceive they have meaning, but I could never tell someone what is going to happen and how or why.

God has given me the understanding after the fact. Then it is a knee-buckling revelation. Completely mind-blowing. But I never could have guessed before the reality what God was showing me because I don't know the future and I'm incapable of distinguishing exactly what the pictures or events mean that He shows me. But afterward, they make perfect sense.

I'd almost suggest that God may have been testing Solomon in 1 Kings when He speaks to Solomon in a dream:

> At Gibeon the LORD appeared to Solomon during the night in a dream, and God said, "Ask for whatever you want me to give you." (1 Kings 3:5 NIV)

The reason I lean in the direction of testing is because of verse 10. *The Lord was pleased that Solomon had asked for this. (1 Kings 3:10 NIV)*

In his unconscious state of sleep, Solomon asked for wisdom to lead God's people. He could have asked for any selfish desire, but instead asked for something good. Because God was so pleased with his request, He gave him incredible wisdom and more. Things he didn't even ask for. He gave him wealth and honor and promised him a long life if he walked in obedience as his father, David, did.

If it was a test, he passed with flying colors.

What if Solomon had asked for something foolish or selfish? Would God have been disappointed instead of pleased? We'll never know because it isn't in the Bible.

But we have our own relationship with God, and how we behave in our dreams is telling. What will we do in our dreams? Will we recognize our bad behavior and stop? Will we wake up, repent, and beg God for forgiveness for what we've just done in our *dreams*? Will we hate our own **sin**? Even in our dreams?

In Psychology, we learn about subconscious work. Hypnotism would be an example of this. There's a space between our conscious mind and our unconscious where our minds can be changed about things. If not changed, then strongly influenced for change to take place.

God is working in our subconscious state through dreams to change our thinking. This is *powerful* work.

He's untangling our thoughts and desires from what's wrong to what's right. Our thinking is often wrong. He makes us aware, and some of this involves dreams.

The word *"mind"* is found 163 times in the Bible (NIV). That's a lot. God knows us inside and out. He knows our thoughts. He knows our intentions when we don't even realize what those may be. We pretend our intentions for doing something are innocent and good. But God knows the underlying issue as to **why** we do certain things and will require change.

Did you know that the brain cleans itself while we sleep?

During deep sleep, toxins are flushed out of the brain through a waste management system called the *"glymphatic system."* While we're dreaming away, our brains are being cleaned, keeping our bodies healthy.

The truth is that God is doing the same thing—cleaning our brains while we sleep.

Only He's doing it spiritually by giving dreams to help us in our spiritual walk. To clean up sin we're unaware of, bringing the sin to our attention through a series of strange dreams. He helps us see where we may be in some sort of bondage through recurring dreams and breaks those chains and sets us free.

All of this is done while we're unconscious.

We're all-in with God, and He's all-in us. The Holy Spirit is within us, working powerfully, though sometimes slowly, to change us inside and out.

He changes what is seen in us and what is unseen because He sees it **all**.

None of us gets a pass on the cleaning, changing, transforming work of God. We all desperately need Him in *every* way. I'm so thankful He is **working** while I'm sleeping.

Sometimes, to be honest, these dreams about sins we don't feel we commit are so humbling it hurts. To be even *more* honest, I didn't really want to include this next series of dreams in this book, but I recognized their importance even if I wish I didn't have to include them. It's embarrassing. I was completely **humbled** by them and horrified by my own behavior in this series of dreams. I hated this part of myself by the end of the dream series and wished what God said wasn't true.

But deep in my heart, I knew what He showed me was true, even if it hurt. I hated the sin He revealed was present deep within me.

The dreams started in 2019. They were vague dreams, and at first, I'd only remember bits and pieces. But when I woke up, I wondered why I was in bed with this person from work. We were snuggled up together like we were deeply in love.

Here is one of those dreams:

> *I was at work in my office, but I was sitting on a bed instead of sitting at a desk. The man at work walked into my office and handed me a golden box with a big gold bow on top. I took the gift from his hands and set it down beside me on the bed. As soon as I set it down, it broke into four parts. The gift was a puzzle.*
>
> *Astonished at the gift breaking apart into four things, I picked up each item and examined it. First, a miniature magnifying glass. Second, a miniature camera. Third, a miniature pair of binoculars, and the last thing was a miniature checkbook register. Each item was made of gold, like the box and bow were. I was mesmerized by the little binoculars and*

put them up to my eyes to look through them. It was
amazing.

I woke up vividly remembering the details of the strange dream. This is a dream I shared with several people. How bizarre.

It put my mind on all the miniature things in the dream and what they could mean. I looked up the definition of each thing, but in all honesty, had no idea what purpose God had in giving me such a strange, interesting dream about mostly things that would help me see. But why were the items all miniature?

At the time, I didn't know. But a couple of years later, I began to make a connection to the dream because I started noticing *small* things in real life that I'd never noticed before. Then one day, God made the purpose of the dream perfectly clear.

But it would take a few years to get to that point. It is tied to my mental health and my emotional well-being. There were things in life I was unable to see, and God gave me the ability to see them. Some of those things were not good things. And they were affecting me in a negative way. I just didn't know it yet.

This golden box dream would be filed under "symbolic" dreams, but it also had to do with healing.

But back to this series of dreams. After quite a while, and *many* dreams, I recognized I was having an affair in these dreams. When I made this connection, I'm not going to lie, I was horrified. I dropped to my knees beside my bed and begged God for forgiveness.

The next dream I had (after the revelation), I expressed how sorry I was and went and got his wife and brought her back to him. I was *disgusted* with myself. I could not believe my bad behavior in these dreams.

A Christian writing friend and I were trying to work on a project at the time, and I couldn't even concentrate on the work when we got together. She knows me well and has heard a lot about my dream life and God. I explained to her about the dream revelation and said, "I'm a dream whore." It seems a little funny to write that after years have passed, but at the time I was heart sick, disgusted, and angry with myself. *How could I have such dreams?*

The truth is, there was something within me that God needed to work out. He revealed sin and allowed it to be shown in dreams to humble me. In real life, I'll run away. I'll leave a place I love over such things. But God wanted me to see I'm not above having an affair, even if it was *just* in my dreams.

What happened because of this dream series?

I developed more compassion for people who have affairs in real life because I understand how it can happen. I know that I can easily do the same thing because God showed me that I'm quite capable. I know I'm not perfect in any way, shape, or form. I'm fallible in almost every way and maybe need to be brought down a peg or two in this area.

Maybe I thought too highly of myself, and God humbled me.

Truth:

> Some dreams will disturb us because they reveal truth we don't want to believe.

Key:

> When we recognize the truth of what God is revealing through the dreams and repent of the sin, we're one step closer to being more like Christ.

> Test me, LORD, and try me, examine my heart and my mind; for I have always been mindful of your unfailing love and have lived in reliance on your faithfulness.
> (Psalm 26:2–3 NIV)

CHAPTER TEN

Secure Attachment

You will be secure, because there is hope; you will look about you and take your rest in safety. (Job 11:18 NIV)

One of the many interesting things that caught my attention in my mental and emotional health journey is that there are different attachment styles. Who knew?

Apparently, we develop one in childhood between birth and two years of age. We're conditioned by our parents and take our cues on how to attach to others. This bond has an impact on our psychological development and relationships.

The attachment styles we develop are one of these:

- Anxious Preoccupied
- Fearful Avoidant
- Dismissive Avoidant
- Securely Attached

If we seek help from a therapist about issues in life, they may want to know about our childhood because our childhood affects our adulthood. We may not realize we have wrong thinking or beliefs we're bringing to our adult life. But we carry our child-hood wounds with us through life. Unless we're able to make the connection between those wounds and what triggers us as adults, we'll continue to have many issues, especially in relationships.

Interesting thing for me to learn, for sure.

Like a good therapist may want to hear about our childhood so they can find out where our issues are coming from, it's the same with God, only He already *knows* our issues. We're the ones who need to know.

So, don't be surprised if God takes us back to childhood in dreams. There may be a childhood wound we've not yet dealt with, and it needs to be revealed and *healed*.

The work of God in our dreams is on a subconscious level. He's doing the work while we're asleep through dreams. This is why hypnotism helps some people stop bad habits like smoking. The subconscious mind needs to be tapped into. We try to stop our bad habits on a conscious level. But it works best when it changes deep within us.

The Mayo Clinic website says the following about hypnotism:

> *Hypnosis is a changed state of awareness and in-creased relaxation that allows for improved focus and concentration. . . . Hypnosis is usually done with the guidance of a health care provider using verbal repetition and mental images. During hypnosis, most people feel calm and relaxed. Hypnosis typi-cally makes people more open to suggestions about behavior changes. Hypnosis can help you gain con-trol over behaviors you'd like to change.*

I find this definition fascinating from a spiritual perspective with God as our Healthcare Worker. He is the Great Physician, so, of course, this is relatable for Christians.

If we think about our relationship with God, we probably have an attachment style. Hopefully, we're securely attached in our hearts and minds. But some Christians may be fearfully attached, anxiously attached, or dismissive in our relationship with God. We're attached —just not in the **best** way.

However, the truth is we're completely **securely attached** through the work of Jesus Christ on the cross. There's nothing that can change an authentic conversion through the Holy Spirit. *Nothing.*

But His work within us is changing us from the inside and drawing us into a more intimate, trusting relationship with Him. God wants us to feel securely attached in every way possible.

He's got us. No doubt. He's not leaving or letting us go.

But in our *insecure* human nature, some Christians may question their salvation. They might wonder if God really loves them after all the terrible things they've done in their past. They might question whether the prayer they prayed was authentic. They may wonder if they need to get rebaptized because maybe they were sprinkled as a child. Or maybe they had a second experience with God (as I did) and wonder if they got their baptism in front of the actual salvation. And truthfully, these are all legitimate things to question and consider. We may want to be rebaptized, and that's a beautiful thing.

But we're the ones who are not feeling secure, even though He has us in His grip. We need to trust Him fully in every area of our lives. We must have **secure** attachment within our own hearts, souls, and minds.

Through our dreams, He works out our insecurities. In doing so, He makes us more like Jesus. We're securely attached because of **Jesus** and only because of Him. The Holy Spirit is within us, removing fear, anxiety, and wrong attitudes we carry through life. The dreams reveal truth, set us free, draw us near, and purify our souls.

Satan causes us all kinds of strife to make us have anxiety or fear. But God draws us near and removes fear. He will demolish anything that causes us not to dwell in safety.

Here is an example of God revealing truth through my own series of childhood dreams:

> *I was in my childhood home helping my mom clean the house. We were in the living room cleaning. Then we were in the laundry room cleaning. I cleaned my bedroom. I cleaned the kitchen. I exhausted myself cleaning my childhood home, taking my cues from my mom on what needed to be cleaned. I went to clean the bathroom, but hesitated at the door; I thought it was a terrible mess in there, and I wouldn't go in and clean it.*

This recurring dream happened over a long period of time. Back when I was dreaming this series of dreams, I just wondered about them and couldn't figure out why I kept dreaming that I was cleaning the house where I grew up.

But Christ is faithful as the Son over God's house. And we are his house, if indeed we hold firmly to our confidence and the hope in which we glory. (Hebrews 3:6 NIV)

Let me add here that we are His "house" and, in a dream series like this one about my childhood, the Holy Spirit is doing some major work cleaning up my **personal** life. Deep-rooted incorrect attachments and wrong thinking developed in childhood.

Eventually, in this dream series, I entered the bathroom. Not on my own, though, because I wouldn't go in there.

Here is the (nearly) final dream:

> *A pastor at a local church marched into the house and took me to the bathroom. He forced me to go inside and showed me the terrible mess. He jerked*

back the shower curtain, and water was spewing everywhere from the shower head. The tub and toilet were filthy. I was embarrassed for him to see the bathroom, and it horrified me to see it for myself. But I faced the reality of the mess that was in there.
I woke up.

The final dream I'm unable to record in this little dream book because it's between me and God. The last dream answered questions about my childhood, and many things made sense after these dreams.

One thing I learned from these dreams is the unhealthy behavior I developed in childhood. I tried hard not to disappoint my parents, and I developed a "people-pleasing" trait. (This was just *one* of my problems. I understood later when I was studying mental and emotional health.)

God saw a tender place that needed to be healed because it was showing up in my adult life. Until I recognized what He saw and acknowledged it, then dealt with it properly, I'd continue allowing the unhealed wound to dictate my actions in adulthood. I was unaware until He brought it to my attention.

Through this experience, when I realized God was working while I was sleeping, it blew my mind that God would bring healing in this way. I love Him even more because I'm amazed and touched that He cared enough to show me things about myself I never even knew.

This is a **secure** attachment.

Truth:

God heals. Like a good psychologist, He knows how to help us heal childhood wounds through recurring dreams about our upbringing.

Key:

Dreaming of a house or parts of a house represents us, as God's children. We are the house because the Holy Spirit resides within us. These would be filed under "bondage-breaking" dreams, but they're also healing because, eventually, God will show us what the true problem is and will bring healing.

It is God who arms me with strength and keeps my way secure. (Psalm 18:32 NIV)

CHAPTER ELEVEN

Study of the Human Mind

L ike I mentioned at the beginning of this book, I **don't** have a degree in Psychology. At least not from an accredited college. But apparently, I went to the school of hard knocks for a Psychology degree and graduated. I say that because it all started with a series of dreams. (Of course . . . .)

Here is one of those dreams:

> *I'm wandering around the town I grew up in and see a guy I work with in real life. I stared at him and questioned how I felt about him. Then, another older man from the church I grew up in grabbed me by my shoulders and turned me around. He was walking me back through town toward the high school. I stopped at some point and stared into a building where a couple of men were singing hymns, and I loved the songs, so I listened for a bit. But soon, he was urging me to go back to high school. He walked me all the way to the door and made me go inside. I sat down by myself on a bench outside the band room. I had no idea why I was there or where I was supposed to go. This serious confusion came over me, and I couldn't*

figure out why I was back at high school or where I should go to class.

I woke up.

There would be many more dreams like this.

Here is another one of those types of dreams:

I'm at high school in the counselor's office. I'd seen my writing friend earlier in the dream, and we were getting ready to graduate. Only the counselor informed me that I didn't have enough credits and couldn't graduate. I was shocked and didn't believe her. But she checked again and said that I was missing two credits in health. Health? The easiest subject of all? How could this be? I was stunned that I wasn't going to graduate with my friends because of the health credit deficit. How did this happen?

I woke up.

I told several people about this strange dream. It was so odd. Why would I be short on having enough graduation credits in health class? What in the world is God trying to tell me? Why am I back in high school? What are these dreams all about spiritually? Obviously, I'm lacking something regarding my health.

Then, sometime later, I had another dream. Here are the details:

My beloved friend shows up in my dream. I'm so happy to see her, and we are laughing about something silly in the dream, then she says, "I'm concerned for your safety." I shrugged and basically was like, "I'm not." Then, she showed me an EpiPen-type thing, and I thought she was going to give herself a shot.

I woke up.

Soon afterward, I had another dream.

> *Again, the same friend shows up. We are walking and talking about life and God. At some point, we were close to a soccer park or basketball court, and a ball hit me on the chest. We continued walking, and she said, "God is sovereign." And I completely agreed and, at some point, in this dream, I got two injections from the EpiPen thing, and then I woke up.*

Again, very soon after this dream, I had another dream about my friend with the EpiPen.

> *I don't remember anything except giving myself four injections with the EpiPen thing. I squeezed the flesh in my leg to get the injection in a good place and then injected myself.*

Of course, I researched why people give themselves shots with an EpiPen.

Toxic shock. People give it to themselves to prevent toxic shock from something that is toxic for them. Wow! Lots of thoughts were running through my mind. What is going on in my life that is causing me not to graduate because I'm short on health credits (spiritually), and I'm giving myself anti-shock medications to prevent toxic shock.

About this time, I was scrolling on social media and a post popped up in my feed. The name of the woman wasn't familiar, but she led online Christian counseling groups, and as I read the information, I decided it wouldn't hurt to go to the free online class, since I was beginning to think I may need some counseling because, evidently, God was trying to tell me something with these dreams. So, I signed up and joined the class online when it was time.

What she said intrigued me, but at the end of the free class, you were offered an opportunity to join their three-month program, and it was kind of expensive. I decided not to join but began listening to her free podcasts. It was soon after this that I heard something I'd never paid any attention to in my life. The person leading the podcast said there are different types of safety. There's physical safety, but there's also emotional and spiritual safety.

That stopped me in my tracks because of what my friend had said in my dream about being concerned about my "safety." It dawned on me, maybe I had a few things to learn in this department, so I joined the online counseling group even though it was expensive.

This was the beginning of me finally earning those two health credits so I could graduate. There was a final dream in this dream series, and it was short and sweet.

> *I was back at the high school in someone's office who had authority. She said, "You've earned your degree in Psychology."*
>
> *I was stunned. I didn't even know I was trying to get a degree in Psychology. My mouth dropped open, and a smile spread across her face, and I perceived she was proud of me.*

I woke up.

By the time I had this dream of earning my degree in Psychology, several years had passed. I completed the online counseling sessions. I joined other online groups and learned about boundaries. I listened to countless podcasts, YouTube videos, went to counseling in person, and read articles and books on emotional safety, boundaries, and others. I'd learned that I had a serious problem being a people-pleaser, and I was somewhat codependent.

I started treating myself better and set some boundaries for my self-protection. I learned about covert narcissism, gaslighting, triangulation, and manipulation, and began to recognize that type of psychological abuse.

I'm not going to lie. I was completely ignorant of these things before I began having a series of dreams about high school and not being able to graduate. I truly did need a couple of health credits so that I could move forward in life in a healthier way. So, yes. I was short on credits in the health department and completely clueless until God brought it to my attention through dreams.

Our **mind** is so important in our relationship with God.

> *Those who live according to the flesh have their minds set on what the flesh desires; but those who live in accordance with the Spirit have their minds set on what the Spirit desires. The mind governed by the flesh is death, but the mind governed by the Spirit is life and peace. (Romans 8:5–6 NIV)*

Our mind, according to Merriam-Webster, is the element, or complex of elements, in an individual that feels, perceives, thinks, wills, and especially reasons.

God never leaves us the way He finds us, thank goodness. He begins a lifelong work of changing us. It is slow-going sometimes (especially for me, it seems). But the work never ends until we're no longer living in the flesh. There'll always be something more needed because the ideal is **Jesus,** and He is perfect.

Dreams can change us, lead us to make changes, and draw us into a deeper relationship with God when we recognize how He's speaking to us through them.

Was it God's will for me to recognize I was people-pleasing instead of God-pleasing?

Absolutely.

Was it God's will for me to recognize my need for boundaries? Most certainly.

No one will ever convince me otherwise. He's worked so powerfully through dreams in my life that I know He must be doing the same with His other children. It's His nature, and it's all over the Bible.

Truth:

God transforms us by the renewing of our minds. Even in our dreams.

Key:

Recognize God in a dream or dreams and be proactive in seeking the purpose of the dream. Be mindful of words or actions in the dream that occur shortly after the dream in real life. Is there a connection? Probably.

You will keep in perfect peace those whose minds are steadfast, because they trust in you.
(Isaiah 26:3 NIV)

CHAPTER TWELVE

Revelation and the Powerful Work of God

"For the revelation awaits an appointed time; it speaks of the end and will not prove false. Though it linger, wait for it; it will certainly come and will not delay. (Habakkuk 2:3 NIV)

God works in powerful ways.

Anyone who has *truly* surrendered to Him and has been a Christian for many years can testify of the strange ways He has worked. Some things are miraculous. There's just no other explanation.

To be completely honest, it surprised me early in my Christian walk when Dad told me to be careful about talking about my dreams. That's because I grew up in a little country church, and we were referred to as "Hardshell Baptists." He was a pastor and had already discovered that many Christians weren't dreamers, and if they were—they didn't think the dreams were from God.

These days, it astonishes me looking back at where I came from to where God has brought me. Many bondages have been broken. **Dreams** were a big part of my journey.

So, I'm not surprised God would use dreams to change the lives of people. I'm not surprised He'd use dreams to *save* us.

According to Nabeel Qureshi (author of *Seeking Allah, Finding Jesus*), approximately 50–70% of former Muslims who are now Christians came partially through visions and dreams.

THIS is what I'm talking about.

This is just one example of the powerful, mighty work of God in our dreams. He works in dreams for many reasons. One of those reasons is to *keep us from the Sword*, as mentioned in the Book of Job.

There are many examples of people having vivid dreams about Jesus speaking to them plainly. Though I do understand why Dad would have given the warning about speaking about dreams, I truly believe it is important to know God still speaks to people this way today. I'm not going to be quiet about what God has done in my dreams. It's too important and too powerful not to share with others. I don't just believe God speaks to us in dreams; I **know** He does.

Like I mentioned, when God gives revelation about a dream, it will probably stun us. It may take many years for the revelation to come. It could be decades. The *key* is to wait and to trust He will give the meaning when the time is right.

We know it took twenty-two years for the reality of Joseph's dream about his family bowing down to come to fruition.

Can you imagine how he must have felt when he realized he was living out the *reality* of the dream God had given him so many years before, when his brothers came for food and bowed before him. Genesis 42 is where this part of the story took place. (I highly recommend reading the story of Joseph in the Bible if you haven't.)

> Although Joseph recognized his brothers, they did not recognize him. Then he remembered his dreams about them and said to them, "You are

spies! You have come to see where our land is unprotected."(Genesis 42:8–9 NIV)

With remembering comes revelation.

I mentioned at the beginning of this little dream book about the first time I recall speaking to Dad about a dream. I was about eleven years old and contemplating joining the church.

Here is the dream:

> *I went in front of the little church to join. I was facing the church pews from where the pulpit was and my dad (though I didn't see him in the dream) would have been standing as the pastor of our little church. There were three older ladies in one church pew facing me. They were sisters. One of the sisters (and I vividly recall which one) was sort of smirking or giggling at the fact that I wanted to join the church. Then she threw a rock and hit me in the eye.* I woke up.

This interaction between Dad and me began a lifelong relationship of discussing dreams. God made me a dreamer, and Dad was one, too. I could go to Dad with dream questions. What a valuable resource God provided in having an earthly father like him. Even in his old age, Dad would ask, "Had any dreams or visions?" He loved to hear about how God worked in my life. He loved to tell me what God had done in his own life. How could I ask for more?

I wish with all my heart Dad was alive now so we could discuss this book. Sadly, he passed away in 2019 from Alzheimer's. The last years of his life were not good for conversation. It was a sad state to see, and I wish I could turn back time and talk with him again about these things before Alzheimer's ravaged his mind.

But such is life, sadly.

Now, back to the childhood dream . . . it's been over forty-five years since I had the dream. Like I mentioned, it may be decades before dream revelation comes. This length of time seems crazy, but the timing couldn't be more perfect.

When the revelation comes for a significant dream, and we've waited years, God may continue to roll out the revelation with smaller revelations until our mind is completely blown and we are drawn to our knees in awe of how He works so powerfully. He will complete what He started in our lives . . . even in our dreams.

> *In all my prayers for all of you, I always pray with joy because of your partnership in the gospel from the first day until now, being confident of this, that he who began a good work in you will carry it on to completion until the day of Christ Jesus. (Philippians 1:4–6 NIV)*

God completely blew my mind when the revelation came regarding the dream about the rock in my eye from childhood.

Here is what happened:

It was a Sunday morning in 2024, and I was watching church online. Pastor R. was teaching on Revelation (which he had been for quite a while), and it was good. Plus, it was Mother's Day. We'd been on vacation, and I stayed home from church trying to recover from being out of town.

I haven't had this type of revelation in a while, and it was amazing it happened during a sermon in the Book of Revelation. (How perfect is that?) As I watched and listened to the sermon, I recalled my recent years of study and how much I'd learned about psychological, emotional, and spiritual manipulation and such things.

The clarity I now enjoy is due to God drawing me to learn what I was missing in the health department. I couldn't fathom how I never thought about these things before or, truthfully, even cared about them. I was blissfully *unaware* of how much these behaviors in other people impacted me. I had no idea my **own** behavior (due to my lack of knowledge) was causing so much trouble in my adult life. It was unhealthy.

But why was I so blind?

Literally, I asked this question in my spirit.

Immediately, the childhood dream with a rock hitting me in the eye flashed through my mind. God brought this dream to remembrance when I asked *why* I was blind. I had not thought about this dream in many years. How interesting.

Could I have been spiritually blinded in childhood by a rock hitting me in the eye when I was thinking of joining the church and about to make a decision to follow Jesus?

How very interesting.

Spiritually blinded to certain types of bad behavior and abuse.

God *allowed* it. Was God showing me a demonic attack even in childhood? Which caused blindness in my vision to see this bad type of behavior in others and myself.

I opened my Bible to read a day or so later. I was reading *The Message* on my phone. What stunned me (again) was the title of the chapter in *The Message*. **TO THROW THE STONE**. Then the chapter blew my mind. It was about throwing the first stone at a sinner. It's the story of the woman caught in adultery who was about to be stoned, but Jesus intervened. He said, "The sinless one among you, go first: Throw the stone." Then he bent down again and wrote some more in the dirt.

I never thought that a childhood dream about a woman throwing a rock and hitting me in the eye had anything to do with **Scripture**.

But there it was right in front of my face. Jesus intervening on her behalf. Saving her from being stoned to death. Honestly, He's done the same for me.

So, with this revelation of the rock being thrown at me caus-ing spiritual blindness as a child, it was also me for whom Jesus was intervening. I was the adulteress in the Book of John. It may be hard for someone who hasn't been living these dreams out for decades to understand. But when I opened my reading and found myself in Scripture and the connection to this childhood dream, it stunned me.

Then the next chapter title in *The Message* was **TRUE BLINDNESS**.

What?

Yes. Exactly.

I turned back the screens on my phone to make sure the for-mer chapter was about the rock being thrown, and it was. The very next chapter is about Jesus healing a blind man. Someone blind since birth. Oh my. Here I am again. Only I was eleven when my spiritual blindness came about from someone throw-ing a rock at me in a little church.

MORE Revelation through God's Word. *Unbelievable.*

As I read this chapter, again, there I am in all my blindness. There, Jesus is stirring up dirt again, mixing it with saliva, and slathering it on my eyes (spiritually). I was in my early fifties when I had the dream about the golden gift box with the minia-ture gold items that all had to do with sight (except for the bank register). Was this dream in 2020 also part of my healing, giving me the ability to see things I couldn't see since childhood? What in tarnation?

I'm the whore and I'm the blind man from (spiritual) birth.

Both apply to me.

In John, chapter 9, the disciples asked Jesus, "Rabbi, who sinned—this man or his parents, causing him to be born blind?" Jesus said, "You're asking the wrong question. You're looking for someone to blame. There is no such cause-effect here. Look in-stead for what God can do."

So, *why* I was blinded is not the right question. But seeing what God can do is what I need to *see*. What God has done is give revelation forty-five years after a dream. He's given me answers and made connections to things I never would have thought of without Him intervening. He gave the dream in such a way that I'd remember it forever. He drove me to my earthly father to discuss the dream. He kept it in my mind for years. He reminded me of the dream at the perfect time to show me why I'd have such a dream. He continued to give revelation about the dream after the initial revelation. I'm stunned by this. Completely stunned.

God **speaks** in the dream. Then, He **answers** with revelation. Then, He **confirms** it through Scripture.

"Look instead for what God can do."

This is how we *know* God has answered us.

Mind blown.

Truth:

> *God gives revelation. He knows how to blow our minds. Experiencing this type of dream revelation draws us closer to Him.*

Key:

> *The key to a dream we can't figure out is to **wait**. God will answer when the time is right.*

> *LORD, I wait for you; you will answer, Lord my God. (Psalm 38:15 NIV)*

CHAPTER THIRTEEN

Dreamer Beware

Why does a dreamer need to beware?
Here are three reasons:

1. **God wants to keep us from pride.**

. *In his pride the wicked man does not seek him; in all his thoughts there is no room for God. (Psalm 10:4 NIV)*

. This sin of pride may be the reason for a string of dreams. Maybe we think too highly of ourselves. Maybe we believe we have things figured out, and we don't rely on God but instead trust ourselves. Maybe, outwardly, we claim to be a Christian, but deep within us, we're following tradition instead of engaging in a personal relationship with Jesus, where truth is found.

. If we, as God's children, have issues with pride (and, certainly, we may be unaware), He will work it out of us in one way or another.

2. **God wants to preserve us from the pit.**

To you, LORD, I call; you are my Rock, do not turn a deaf ear to me. For if you remain silent, I will be like those who go down to the pit. Hear my cry for

mercy as I call to you for help, as I lift up my hands
toward your Most Holy Place. Do not drag me away
with the wicked, with those who do evil, who speak
cordially with their neighbors but harbor malice in
their hearts. (Psalm 28:1–3 NIV)

. A pit may literally mean someone dug a pit in the dirt
somewhere. But figuratively, it basically means hell. God
doesn't want us to go to hell. He went to great lengths to
prevent it. He sent His Son, Jesus, to pay our sin debt in
full, which Jesus did willingly because He was obedient
to His Father, so that we can go to heaven with Him instead. We're bound for hell, in case you're unaware, until
we're saved by the blood of Jesus Christ. He intervenes
and changes our eternal destination when we surrender
and place our trust in Him for what He's done for us.

. Also, God gives dreams to **lost** people. Pharaoh was (most
likely) lost, but God gave him two disturbing dreams
which Joseph was able to interpret. This is just one example in the Bible, but there are others. These days, there
are *many* who proclaim Jesus came to them in dreams and
that's how they **met** Him. That's how they were drawn to
Him and were saved.

3. **God wants to keep our lives from perishing.**

The Lord is not slow in keeping his promise, as some
understand slowness. Instead he is patient with you,
not wanting anyone to perish, but everyone to come
to repentance. (2 Peter 3:9 NIV)

. Just like God doesn't want us to go to hell (we will go
there of our own free will by denying Jesus), similarly, He
also doesn't want us to perish. In Christ, we can have an
abundant, beautiful life. Not because we don't have any

problems, because we most definitely will have them, but with our growing faith in God as we develop a deeper relationship with Him, the problems are less difficult to bear. We will find ourselves trusting Him more as we know Him and love Him more intimately. This growth process makes our life problems somewhat less taxing because we know the power of God in our lives and that He has good purposes in the places He takes us.

In conclusion, God wants to keep us from pride. He wants to preserve us from the pit. He wants to keep our lives from perishing. He loves us beyond comprehension.

The God given dream can be because He doesn't want us to go to the pit (or to hell). The dream could be because we're full of pride, relying on our own perception of the world and our own perception of who God is, instead of getting the truth of who He is from the Bible.

He sent His only beloved Son to die in our place on the cross, bearing the sin of the world, to make a way for us to be in a right relationship with God. Jesus is the only way to heaven. Though some in this world deceive many with false gods and false religions. Many will end up in the pit due to the deception of Satan.

When we think we're a pretty *good* person and that's enough to get us there, we're deceived. When we think Jesus isn't really God, we're deceived. When we rely on what our parents taught us or what they believe instead of our own intimate, genuine relationship with Jesus, we're deceived.

If God is giving us dreams (symbolic dreams, prophetic dreams, or any kind of dream that draws us to question what in the world the dream is about), He may be trying to get our attention. He wants a *relationship* with us. He loves us. He wants us to know Him and love Him, too. He wants us with Him in **heaven** for eternity.

But He also wants to lead us through our daily life, relying on Him exclusively.

He *is* God.

The *only* God.

Powerful.

Mighty.

All-knowing.

Present everywhere at the same time.

The Holy Spirit indwells us when we surrender our will to His will. We give Him access to every square inch of our heart, soul, mind, and body. Nothing is hidden anyway. He knows our thoughts. He knows our intentions. He knows our hearts. He begins His incredible work making us like His Son, who was in complete surrender to His Father, all the way to death on a cross.

For us.

Some Christians gave their life to Christ as a child. They were baptized. They went to church often or, possibly, most Sundays. But they have no relationship with Jesus because they've never surrendered entirely to Him. Sadly, the churches may well be filled with lost people who think they're saved because they quoted a prayer and were baptized as children.

But were they ever baptized and indwelled with the *Holy Spirit*?

Indwelling is *life*-changing.

After this experience in my own life, my thoughts turned to God 80% of the time. It seemed everything I thought sifted through a God filter.

I fell madly in love with Jesus Christ. I became consumed by Him. I read the New Testament more than anything else because I found Him there. His life poured out for me.

Me.

Unreal.

For the first time in my life, I felt the soul-satisfying forgiveness of sins I'd wrestled with for years. They were forgiven. I didn't need to carry their weight any longer. My spirit slipped free from those chains binding me through the power of the Holy Spirit, speaking truth to me about all Jesus had done for me. Relief and joy abounded at these wonderful revelations coming to me from Him.

Dream Discernment

The truth is, we must use discernment when we try to interpret a dream. We may not be able to interpret it at all until later.

Here is a simple strategy for seeking the meaning of a dream.

- **Write it down.** Every detail is important, even if it seems strange or insignificant. Email it to yourself for a record of the date. Or, even better, keep a journal for recording significant dreams. Be sure to note everything about the dream and also anything going on in real life that may have caused the dream to occur.
- **Seek Scripture.** Whatever elements of the dream were significant, search a Bible application online for those specific things. Note in your journal (if you're keeping one) what Scripture jumps out for you when searching the Bible.
- **Ponder the dream.** Think about the dream. You'll probably naturally do this anyway, because if it is a God dream, certainly, this is one of the purposes of the dream. God *wants* us to think about the meaning of our dreaming.
- **Share the dream with a believer.** It is helpful to share the dream with a fellow believer who is also a dreamer, if

possible. They may see meaning in the dream right away. Like my friend immediately shared an insightful Scripture about being set free from the fear of death when I shared my death dream with her many years ago.

- **Pray.** Of course, we should talk to God about our dream. At least, ask and silently wait for an answer. We can ask as many times as we like. God wants us to go to Him with our inquiries, especially when He's the One giving us the interesting or strange dream that is causing us to think about Him, drawing us to Scripture and prayer.

- **Wait.** The hardest of all, I'm afraid. The meaning of the dream may come quickly or it may take many years. But keeping good records, pondering the dream, studying Scripture, seeking God, and praying are all good practices.

Also, it might be hard not to look up the meaning of dream elements in the glossary of a dream book or dream website. There's nothing wrong with that, in my opinion. But as I mentioned previously, our dreams are personal.

They're between God and us. They're about us most often. They're about drawing us into a deeper relationship with Him.

God is speaking.

It's our job to listen and learn.

Sweet Dreams and Rest

This is not about dreams but rest.

When we're going through a stressful time due to life changes or uncertainty, we can become exhausted from lack of sleep due to unsettled feelings in our spirit. We may become caught in the cycle of waking up at 3:00 a.m.

That's one place where God *works*.

It's the symbolic hour of the finished work of Christ on the cross. When death was defeated. When our sin debt was paid in full. If we find ourselves awakened repeatedly at this hour for a long period of time, God is most likely doing *something* in our lives.

If you're unfamiliar with this truth, let me fill you in. I heard about it from Dad. I'm sure it came up in one of our many conversations about God. It gave me great peace when he explained it because I was afraid it was something other than God causing me to wake up at that time, and it left me unsettled. I wasn't sure how to handle it. Here is what he told me, and it's true. (You can Google it.)

What does the Bible say about waking up at 3:00 a.m.?

In the Gospel of Luke, we find something interesting.

*It was now about noon, and darkness came over the whole land until **three** in the afternoon, for the sun stopped shining. And the curtain of the temple was torn in two. Jesus called out with a loud voice, "Father, into your hands I commit my spirit." When he had said this, he breathed his last. (Luke 23:44– 46 NIV)*

It doesn't matter if it was a.m. or p.m. when it occurred. The *time* is what is significant.

Three o'clock is when the veil was torn in two and Jesus gave up His spirit to *save us*. He suffered up until three o'clock bearing our shame, humiliation, and sin. His death, marked by the same hour, is making a way for us to be right with God again. To be able to communicate with Him without a veil of separation.

Of course, demons probably celebrated at this time because of His death. They aren't all-knowing like God, so I believe they were clueless He was about to bust open a tomb in three days.

So, now, my spirit rejoices when I wake up at 3:00 a.m.

Thank you, Jesus.

However, not only did God finish the work on the cross at that time, but He may be working in our lives and waking us up at the same time as a sign of *His work* in our lives. Sometimes, we're awakened by a dream. If so, recall the details and write them down if you struggle to remember. But I seem to remember most God dreams because they are stamped into my brain, and I'm amazed by them.

When we finally get some good *restful* sleep, we make peace with whatever God is doing. Peace comes from resting in the work of God. *Blissful* peace.

It's okay whether it's this thing or that thing . . . either way, it's okay. We're in the middle of God's will when we're lined up with Him, and we're okay with whatever He wants to do in our lives.

He will guide us.

He's in complete control.

Wait in faith.

Rest in the work of God in our lives and find the place of blissful peace, knowing He has our best interests at heart.

Sweet dreams, my friend.

> *Truly my soul finds rest in God; my salvation comes from him. Truly he is my rock and my salvation; he is my fortress, I will never be shaken. (Psalm 62:1–2 NIV)*

www.ingramcontent.com/pod-product-compliance
Lightning Source LLC
Chambersburg PA
CBHW032013040426
42448CB00006B/618